Rental Property Millionaire

The Ultimate Crash Course On Rental Property Investing

responsibility of the recipient reader. Under no circumstances will any legal responsibility or blame be held against the publisher for any reparation, damages, or monetary loss due to the information herein, either directly or indirectly.

Respective authors own all copyrights not held by the publisher.

Table Of Contents

Introduction:
Creating a New Business
Model

I want to thank you and congratulate you for purchasing the book *Rental Property Millionaire: The Ultimate Crash Course on Rental Property Investing.* In the following chapters, we'll be discussing the strategies, techniques, and skills used by experienced real estate investors.

BONUS:
Revolutionary Credit Repair Secrets

And as a special thank you to my readers, I am giving away free copies of my book- **Revolutionary Credit Repair Secrets- Cardinal Rules to Get You a Perfect Credit Score.** You will receive outstanding tips to improve your credit score, which will assist you both in Real Estate Investing and in your financial health matters in general.

To get instant access to this book and more awesome resources, check out the link below:

**https://mccordpublishing.leadpages.co/
real-estate-investing**

As an added bonus, subscribers will be given a chance to get exclusive sneak peeks of upcoming books and discounts that will not be available to the general public. You will also have the opportunity to obtain free copies of my books with no strings attached. Don't worry, we treat your e-mail with the respect it deserves. We will not spam you and that's a promise!

What We Will Cover on Rental Property Investing:

As you journey through all the incredible opportunities that residential and commercial real estate investing offers, you'll be better prepared to address the questions you must be having at this time in your career, such as.

- Which is the better investment, residential or commercial properties? Or, should I do both?

- Should I get a real estate license as an investor?

- How do I "hardline negotiate" yet still preserve my relationships?

- What are some unique investment opportunities in today's market?

- When partnering with other professionals, how can I sweeten the deal to get exclusive perks and privileges?

As you examine our proven strategies, you'll better understand how to develop a cash flow that requires little to no out-of-pocket expenses with your initial purchases, and you'll learn how to take advantage of capital appreciation, depreciation, and tax benefits that you may have previously missed. You'll also see how the industry "players" leverage their investments to maximize their returns.

If you've previously only dabbled in real estate investments, you'll find that going "all in" comes with a whole new set of rules and winners. Today's big investment market is ripe for ambitious entrepreneurs, but you might not be welcomed in with open arms by your competitors. Instead, you'll learn how to earn your way in by being prepared for all the possible successes and setbacks, and getting financially and educationally fit to run with the big dogs.

If you have been running your investing endeavors by a "fly-by-the-seat-of-your-pants" method, be ready for a shake-up. It's time to create a business plan and model that will enable you to identify and pursue your niche market.

The decisions you make now will create a portfolio of investments that will allow you to expand and explore new investments in unique ways and in unusual markets. So, let's get started, shall we?

It Doesn't Have to Be an Either or Proposition

Some investors have limited themselves to residential properties, which include single-family homes and multiple housing developments. The reasons for this can be as predictable as because that is the type of properties in which they are most familiar. Many of these entrepreneurs began as experienced Realtors® who saw the advantages to owning rental properties. It was an easy transition to use their skills and knowledge in residential properties and build their investment portfolios on types of properties in which they had proven themselves successful.

If you are experiencing all the financial benefits you had hoped for with your residential investments, then continue with what works well for you. However, if you are hungry to spread your financial wings, to overcome new challenges and experience new breakthroughs in your investment business, then it's time to develop an exciting new business model and adopt proven principles that will broaden your scope.

Creating A New Business Plan

When you began investing, your business plan, if you had one, was probably elementary. You looked for a rental property, purchased it, rehabbed it, rented or sold it, and then started the process all over again. While that may work with five properties or less, it's insufficient for high-volume investing. Now you need a real business plan. Here are some of the things it should include.

Mission Statement:

A mission statement should be...

- In writing

- Clear and concise

- State your purpose

- Define what differentiates you

- Identify the benefits you provide

Goals:

Your goals should...

- Be in writing using specific language (including figures & percentages)

- Have deadlines (date of completion)

- Be measurable (you'll know you have succeeded when...?)

- Include steps taken to achieve success

- Be celebrated when achieved

Strategies:

What will you do to reach success?

- Do you plan on flipping the property? Or selling it?

- Will you make a lease purchase?

- Will this property be a short or long-term rental?

- Will it be an event or seasonal rental?

- How will you purchase it? Loan? Private Money? Crowdfunding?

- How will your team or partner be involved? Or do you plan on working alone?

- What are your limits? High, low, and desired figures?

- What is your defined exit strategy for each property?

- Have you done your due diligence?

What is your market for each property?

- Low or high-income property?

- Commercial or residential?

- Local or long distance investment

- How will you find your buyers/sellers/renter?

Who makes up your team?

- Will you use an investing partner for all properties? Some? None?

- Do you have professionals on your team? CPA? Attorney? Realtors®? Contractors? Title Officers? Mortgage people? Property Manager? Insurance Agent? Handyman? Decorator/Stager?

There are many decisions to make as you are developing your new business plan, and that's the beauty of doing one—making concrete plans for each investment. You might change your mind and your team members frequently, so consider your new plan a foundation that you can build upon for every investment in your portfolio.

Your new business plan should give you direction and guidance from which to draw from but realize that real estate investing is a changing business that blows with the wind of the market and its trends. Your new plan should include all the ingredients that give you a taste of well-thought-out real estate investing.

Additionally, the art of Rental Property Investing is only one component of Real Estate Investing. Our books tackle these other components such as **Flipping Houses for Profit**, **Real Estate Investing,** how to become a **Real Estate Agent,** and even a step by step guide to achieving an **excellent Credit Score** to get you the loan with the best rates. And for anyone interested in the **Tiny House Movement**, we have books on that subject as well!!

Please check out our Amazon Author Page to find selections like this!

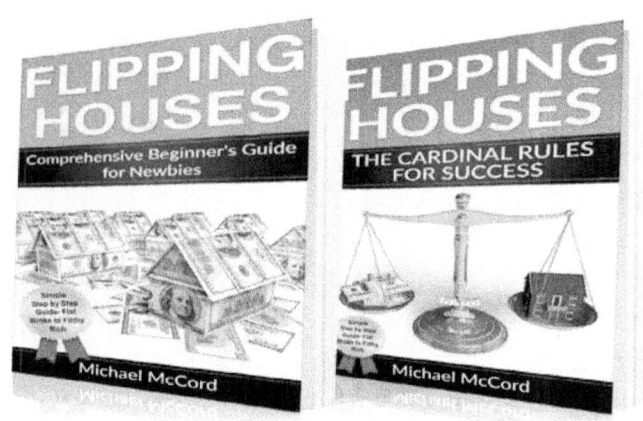

https://www.amazon.com/ Michael-McCord/e/B01LYIFPLO/ ref=dp_byline_cont_ebooks_1

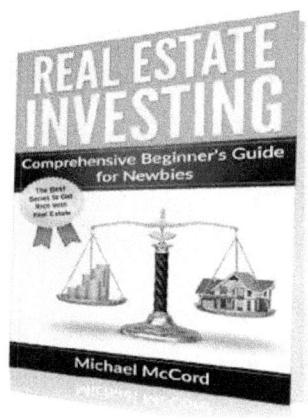

https://www.amazon.com/
Michael-McCord/e/B01LYIFPLO/
ref=dp_byline_cont_ebooks_1

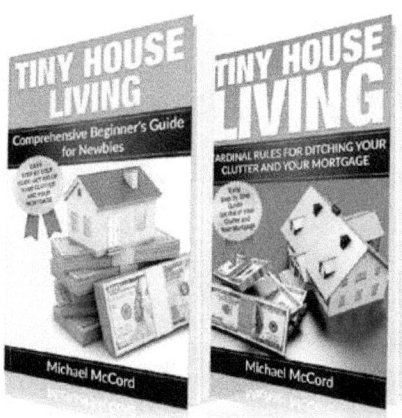

https://www.amazon.com/
Michael-McCord/e/B01LYIFPLO/
ref=dp_byline_cont_ebooks_1

There are plenty of books on this subject on the market, thanks again for choosing this one! We will not disappoint!

Chapter 1:
Commercial, Residential, or Both?

There is no right or wrong type of real estate in which to invest; it boils down to preference. What limits your potential profits is not whether the property is commercial or residential, but, rather, can you be single-minded and focused on your goal and work your plan? It is the opinion of many, that people who try to invest in both residential and commercial spread themselves too thin and cannot maintain their market edge in either area. Because these two areas of real estate are so diverse, it requires investors who decide to do both to wear many hats.

Ask yourself—how big is your head? If you have the confidence, skills, knowledge, and guts to do both, you might just be the exception to the rule. To help you make an informed decision, both types of investments will be presented. You be the judge!

Advantages of Investing in Residential Real Estate

What is meant by residential investing is both single-family and multiple family properties, such as houses, duplexes, and small apartment complexes. There are five primary advantages for investing in residential real estate.

1. ***Investing in residential real estate usually doesn't require as much initial or reserve capital.***

   Because the properties are less expensive, and you are dealing with individual sellers and buyers, the money you'll need for an initial investment is less. Also, most residential property maintenance or updating is not as expensive, and you can build those costs into the lease agreement. For instance, you can write into the rental agreement that the renters will be responsible for the first $200 of repairs of major appliances, air conditioning unit, heating system, etc. Of course, if repairs are necessary due to renters' negligence, they will be responsible for the entire cost of the damage or repair.

There are always ways to avoid these things when investing in commercial real estate. For example, you may want to create an investment group, which will substantially divide your initial costs and ongoing liabilities. With a triple net, commercial lease, the cost of maintenance is reduced to a negligible amount. So, if you are leaning toward commercial investments, don't let these two things stop you.

2. *It is much easier to compute the value of residential properties as opposed to commercial ones.*

With residential properties, primarily single-family homes, the necessary information you need to set the appropriate value of a home is.

- What similar homes in the area have sold for in the last three to six months to determine the price you can expect to pay. If you're a good negotiator and have a motivated seller, you can purchase the home for much less.

- What repairs need to be done, and what will it cost for your contractor or handyman to complete them? You will also need to know the time of completion, as this can weigh into your year-end profits.

- Once the repairs and updates have been made, how much will the home be worth?

- What will the home rent for when the repairs and updates have been completed?

On the other hand, computing the value of commercial property is more challenging, with many more variables. Most commercial properties are valued using the income approach. You must first know the market's cap rate. Then you find the annual profit of the commercial property and multiply it by the cap rate to determine value. Cap rates vary depending on the type of commercial property, the location, region, tenant stability, lease length, and condition of assets. Low prices on a piece of commercial property might not be such a smokin' deal if that price reflects a poor tenant or uncertain market. The investor might also be fooled by a dishonest owner who is stretching the numbers to make the property look more appealing, and you're left holding the bag.

3. *Investing in residential real estate can be a safer bet if the market tanks.*

It's a numbers game. We all need a place to live, and many can't afford to own in a down market—so you can usually get higher rent and a larger pool of viable tenants. It can also be more challenging for residential buyers to qualify for a loan in a down market, so renting is their only option, which will prove beneficial for the residential investor.

Down markets can be killers for the commercial investors. Tenants decide to close up shop and work from home to avoid the costs of expensive commercial leases. Commercial loans are harder to obtain when the market gets tight, so people can't afford to open a business. Because everything works off supply and demand, the more spaces available, the lower the rents. Unfortunately, all this comes at a time when commercial investors need more money because of vacancy rates. The risks can be astronomical for commercial investors when they are forced to sell in a down market. Property value is down, and buyers are few.

4. Residential loans are easier to get and longer in duration.

As an investor, qualifying for a loan on residential property might require a bit more as an initial down payment, but the qualifying terms are usually much easier, especially if you plan on keeping the property for two to five years.

Commercial properties are amortized over a shorter period, with a hefty balloon payment due in five or ten years. Many commercial investors are then forced to take on a partner, refinance, find private financing, or sell the property to satisfy the balloon payment. A precarious position, indeed!

5. Residential leases are easier to understand.

Most of the time it's a straightforward lease that includes the following terms and conditions.

- Tenant names and contact information

- Terms of lease

- Duration of lease

- Monthly rent payment

- Amount of security and cleaning deposits

- Pets allowed or not allowed—deposit to be charged for pet

- Number of people living on the property

- Access instructions for inspection purposes

- Maintenance of property and appliances

- Repairs stipulations

- Late fees

- Grounds for Termination

- No illegal activities

Advantages of investing in Commercial Real Estate

There are additional concerns when investing in commercial real estate, but there are also bigger benefits, such as the following.

1. *Commercial investments usually provide greater returns.*

   Investors who are knowledgeable enough to choose a suitable commercial property and value it properly, stand a better chance to make greater returns on their initial investment.

2. *Investors in commercial property usually have long-term tenants with fewer daily hassles.*

   The nagging daily issues that plague residential investors are not applicable to commercial investors. Most commercial investors use a triple-net lease, which makes the tenant responsible for all maintenance problems within their individual space. Because commercial leases are for longer timeframes, there are not the constant negotiations of rents.

Commercial leases also come with an automatic annual or semi-annual rent increase, which allows the investor to collect higher rents without having to renegotiate the contract. The lease is capped per year, but it does cover increases in taxes. Also, the tenant is required to carry their own space and liability insurance, which relieves the commercial investor.

3. Commercial investors buy into a money-making proposition.

When commercial investors make an investment, they most likely already have some long-term, stable anchor tenants who are providing income. That's why it is called income-producing property. If you do your due diligence, and the market is stable, you should not have any issues acquiring good tenants. In a down market, commercial property will cost less money, but the leasing situation can get dicey.

Many commercial investors who have balloon payments also offer their paper mortgages to other investors. Or, they bring in investing partners to share in the costs. Commercial endeavors often attract investors with deeper pockets, so partnering with another investor alleviates some of the financial burdens or frees up money for other investments.

4. *Commercial investors have less competition.*

The area of commercial property that has the least competition is that under five million dollars. It is the "tweener" investment—too large for most residential investors, and too small an amount for most commercial investors. So, when you contact owners of commercial property in this price range, you probably won't have ten more investors ahead of you and behind you, waiting for their turn at the seller. The challenge is to find a commercial property under five million that will give you a significant ROI.

5. *Commercial investing is less emotional.*

Residential owners always tend to think their home is worth more than it is, even when they see the comps. They consider it a personal offense when you devalue their home, or angry when you come in with a low-ball offer. They resent negotiating the sales price, even when they expect it from an investor. In fact, many homeowners have a negative view of an investor purchasing their home.

Commercial property owners act quite differently. It's usually not an emotional transaction for them—it's all about business. When you negotiate a good buy, they secretly admire your tenacity and market knowledge when you show them your figures. Although placing a value on commercial property is more complicated, owners take the numbers at face value and are less likely to question your research. Not that they're not going to hold out for another investor willing to pay more money, but you're not going to experience an emotional meltdown. They're just hoping you'll accept their valuation and not be one of the determined investors who does his or her homework.

What About Working Both Sides of the Fence?

Working both residential and commercial properties presents many challenges. In fact, most investors are typically attracted to one type of real estate or the other, depending on their personalities. As I said before, Realtors® must wear many hats when doing just one type of transaction; multiply that by two and that's a lot of balloons to keep up in the air at once.

If you are currently investing in residential and would like to try commercial, the best thing to do is to work with another commercial investor. It can be difficult to find a commercial investor who is willing to educate you, but if you have something to offer, then perhaps they will consider it. For example, if you are prepared to do a lot of the running for a while, some of the paperwork, and perhaps become a financial partner in an investment with them to learn the ropes, then maybe you'll get an "inside track" advantage.

Most commercial investors don't invest in residential property, so trading knowledge is not an option. Herein is the issue, finding someone who can walk you through some transactions until you feel confident to go it on your own. However, planning to work both residential and commercial is more than most investors want to tackle. Most will tell you that it's more advantageous to choose between the two and focus your energies on where your expertise can make you the most return on your investment.

Chapter 2:
To Be—Or Not to Be
a Licensed Realtor®

The juries out when it comes to the question of whether to become a licensed Realtor® when you are an active investor. There are clearly advantages and disadvantages on both sides. If you are a licensed Realtor® and an investor, you apparently believe there is an advantage to getting licensed. Investors who are not licensed argue the point of the necessity of licensing with their reasoning, as well. Each viewpoint has good reasoning for and against being licensed, so you'll need to judge for yourself.

Why Get Your Real Estate License?

Even investors who are not licensed admit there are some real advantages to becoming a Realtor®. One primary reason is that you have access to the Multiple Listing Service (MLS). Not only will this make you privy to every property available in your area, but it also gives you some very valuable information that you might otherwise not have. Although it is mostly used for residential listings, there are some commercial ones there as well. Here are the perks the MLS offers.

- All the homes that are for sale and that have sold in the area. This means that you can quickly run comps to discover the value of the property.

- It also lets you know how many days the property has been on the market. This is a crucial piece of information. It indicates whether the owners have it overpriced, or if they could be difficult sellers. You can see if the property is in poor condition, or perhaps it's in an undesirable area. What it means to investors is that it could be ripe for a price reduction and a sound investment. The longer a home stays on the market, the more anxious sellers might be to be done with it and move on to their next home.

- You can also see what features the home contains. Comparing the home to others in the area will let you know what is selling and how long it takes them to sell. By looking at the features, you'll know if the home has a "WOW" factor. This is a vital thing that many investors overlook. Because investors look at the home as a business opportunity, they are not emotionally attached or influenced by floor plans and appearances. However, you can bet your renters or buyers will make their decisions emotionally—based on the WOW factor. That's what buyers do, they make their decision emotionally and justify them logically. What they want is something investors don't think about when buying property. They are looking for the WOW!

Most Realtors® will be the first to share the truth of that statement. When they've shown buyers a gazillion homes and finally, in frustration, asked them what they were looking for, the buyers couldn't verbalize their wants. They simply said, "I'll know it when I see it." That, my friend, is the expressed need to have something that makes the home remarkable, something memorable, something that makes them throw out their previous list and settle on a home that isn't at all what they first described to their Realtor®. They're looking for the WOW in their next home.

It can be quite frustrating for the agents because nobody knows what that WOW factor is until they've seen it. The best way to ensure your property will have the WOW factor is to create it yourself. We'll be talking about how to do that when we cover staging for the sale or rental. For now, just know that it helps if you have a little built-in WOW.

- The MLS also gives you the parcel number of the home and loan information. This too is invaluable information for the investor. This often lets you know how much equity the seller holds. Of course, this is not going to tell you if the sellers obtained a second loan sometime after the initial sale, but at least you get some of the financial histories. If you think there might be some equity in the property, perhaps the sellers would be willing to offer private financing or exceptional terms. Or, maybe they would take less down or pay the closing costs.

  In many of the listings, a motivated seller will indicate the terms they are willing to take. While that might not be as important to a regular buyer, it's gold to an investor who is mining for a property at the lowest price with the least out-of-pocket expense.

- The MLS also lets you know the age of the property and the property tax amount. If the home is new, your tax amount may not have been properly set yet, but if the house is over three years old, it's probably not going to experience a substantial increase in the next year or two.

- It also lets you know the names of the sellers, or if the property is in a trust. This too is great information to have. If the home is a part of a trust, it could be that the family has inherited the home and wants to get it off their back. This presents an exciting opportunity for an investor.

Let me share with you an interesting story. I once had the opportunity to purchase a property that was held in the name of *The Lewis Family Trust*. I also noticed that on a floor tile in the corner of the living room of the home was written *Lewis Family*. Being the curious person I am, and believe me, that is an asset to have as an investor, I began to ask some innocent sounding questions when I talked to the seller's Realtor®. I mentioned that there was a tile in the living room that I found interesting that read *The Lewis Family*, and how quaint it was.

Before I go any further, let me also share with you that I had some real misgivings about purchasing the home because it was priced to market, but it needed significant work. If the seller wasn't willing to reduce the price, then

I questioned whether I should purchase the home. What it did have going for it was the area. It was a great area that was a little older but had retained its value.

Back to my innocent conversation with the Realtor®. When I mentioned that my buyers thought it quaint, the Realtor® said, "Oh yes; the home belonged to T. W. Lewis. He purchased it for his mother, who recently passed. Well, as innocent as that piece of information sounds, T. W. Lewis is a builder of luxury homes, and now my game plan changed. Instead of asking for a huge reduction in price, I asked for all the repairs to be done by his contractors, and they were many. I got a remodeled kitchen, rehabbed bathrooms, new flooring, a rebuilt backyard patio with a barbecue, a new tile roof, new air conditioner, and the yard landscaped.

The remodel was easy for him to complete with his contractors. What would have taken me weeks was accomplished in a matter of days, and the craftsmanship and furnishings were what would have gone into a luxury home. Those, after all, were the types of homes he built. It saved me a tremendous amount of time and money. I rented the property for much more because of all the upgrades and sold it seven years later for an incredible profit. All of that because I chatted with the Realtor®. I showed interest in the home and asked some curious little questions that provided me with an incredible amount of information. Which brings me to my next point; it's all about the agents.

- The MLS also lets you know the agents and their contact information, and whether the property is vacant. It nice to find a vacant home, because you can preview without the scheduling hassles.

If the MLS were the only advantage to getting your real estate license, that would be enough to convince many investors, but there are a few other things. Licensed investors also receive information that could save them in legal situations. As much as disclosures can be a pain, don't think that you don't have to disclose if you are not a licensed Realtor®. Anytime you purposefully defraud someone because you do not disclose something about the property that could influence their purchasing decision, you could be held accountable for that. So, if an investor says they don't want to get licensed because they would then have to disclose everything about the property. You should be doing that anyway.

The Downside to Being Licensed

There is paperwork up the ying yang! It's not as simple as just contacting the sellers and letting them know you're interested in buying their home. Since it takes some time to become a real estate broker, as a Realtor®, you will be playing by somebody else's rules. All your transactions will need to be submitted to your designated broker for approval, and it's his or her license on the line. So, they will be looking over your agreements closely. In other words, until you obtain your broker's license, you will be subject to the requirements of your designated broker and the brokerage. This can be quite limiting, especially because many of them don't understand the needs of investors.

They operate with a different set of requirements, and most of those are designed to protect themselves and their brokerage, which is understandable. However, the whole investor endeavor is about taking risks, and some of the risks mean you walk on the edge of what many brokers consider ethical. Not that you are dishonest, just smart. You have a business model that is worlds apart from that of the standard Realtor®. So, if you are going to get licensed, find a firm that welcomes investors. Ask some investors you know where they hang their licenses, and if they are given the freedom necessary to make profitable deals.

Because firms are as concerned with protecting their behinds as much as with making the deals, the paperwork created is phenomenal. The purchase agreement is nine to ten pages; the listing agreement is three. It is often frowned upon to represent both the seller and buyer in an agreement and so to protect them you must have a Dual Agency Agreement authorized by everybody and their brother. There are pages of disclosures that can be quite tedious to complete, and every time you make one small time change or vendor change, there's another addendum to complete, have signed by all parties, and submitted to your designated broker.

If you do decide to get licensed, you will need the support of a spouse or a transaction coordinator to help you with all the paperwork demands. However, work the numbers. You could pay for several assistants by what you'll make in commissions with a real estate license, especially if you are investing in upper-end properties. The higher the price of the property, the more money you'll make in commissions. After all the paperwork, you'll be saying to yourself—there is a God!

Belonging to the National Association of Realtors® (NAR) and a local Board or Realtors® are also useful tools to have as an investor. Your dues will cost several hundred a year, but if that is going to make or break you, perhaps you should be doing something else besides investing in real estate. You'll get so much information through your local boards, including any legal changes or legislation, and practices of other top producers in the industry that might be useful for you to know.

I've heard it said by investors that do not want to be licensed that the hours it takes to get licensed is a burden for them. While some classes are not applicable to investors, the overall information makes it time well spent. Some cities offer a crash course that only takes two to three weeks, and with a little study you're ready for your state exam. If you go into it with an open mind instead of feeling as if you are wasting your time, you'll be surprised at what you will learn and how the education will benefit you later.

If you get your license, you can refer buyers and sellers who contact you to represent them as a Realtor® to other agents and received referral fees. Or, you can waive the fees and create some excellent relationships with other Realtors® that will far outweigh the small referral fees you could have collected. They'll be contacting you with sellers who are desperate to sell, and you could find a reduced property, in good condition, in a dynamite neighborhood. You can create valuable relationships with talented Realtors®. It's an excellent symbiotic relationship where everybody wins.

As in all investor decisions, do your homework before making the choice of whether to obtain your real estate license. To give you both sides of the picture, ask investors who have their license and those who don't, what motivated their decisions. Then, it's up to you. You'll need to determine what works best with your business plan.

Chapter 3:
Creating the WOW Factor

As much as investors pride themselves on detaching from the emotional part of the purchase or sale, there are times when they must re-engage. If your plan is to flip the property or rent it quickly for more money, you need to appeal to the buyers and tenants' emotions. Just this one thing will make you so much more money. So, let's talk about how to do that.

The first mistake many investors make is that they try to be all things to all people. If you are determined to handle every aspect of the sale, you'll need to be an investor, Realtor®, banker, contractor, handyman, decorator, administrator, transaction coordinator, landscaper, and goodness knows what else. Spreading yourself this thin will not make you more money; it will cost you in time lost revenue, when you're not just doing what you do best. If we can agree that focusing on investing should be your goal, then how can you possibly find the time to create WOW in your properties?

I'll tell you! Leave it to the experts. It doesn't take that much more money or time to transform your properties from outdated to outstanding.

What it does take is a team of experts who know they will get ongoing work from you if they are good at what they do, do it in quick time, and are willing to reduce their rates for your business. There are plenty of experts in their fields who are ready and waiting for your call.

Who Are the Experts You'll Need on Your Team?

When you are looking for talented people, refuse to settle for ordinary people who might consider themselves good at their craft but have no proof. For example, when you hire a contractor, find one who is licensed and bonded. One of the ways to do this is to go to the Registry of Contractors and find someone who is retired but still wants to keep his hands in the business. They would most likely be willing to help you out for a fraction of the cost, and they'll have plenty of references. The others you'll need on your team are as follows.

- A Mortgage Company (Preferably, the owner will also be the loan officer and processor). If it is a small company, you'll be in touch with the decision maker, and they'll be willing to work with your demands as an investor. Make sure they can do construction loans and have available creative financing; there will be times when you need it. There is a big difference between a mortgage company and a mortgage broker. The mortgage broker is one who has a portfolio of leading lenders who offer a broad range of specialty loans. Mortgage brokers are the way to go; it will cost you less time and usually less money.

- If you decide to get licensed, go with a firm which houses a lot of investors. They will be accustomed to handling your needs, and they won't fear a little creativity in the agreements. These types of firms also have outstanding Realtors® to whom you can refer, and they don't require you to attend weekly office meetings or jump through as many hoops as other more traditional firms. In fact, they cater to your needs. You'll still have to abide by the regulations of the Department of Real Estate, but those rules will serve to protect you as well make sellers and buyers feel good about working with you.

- An outstanding title officer can save your behind when it comes to investing, even if you decide not to become licensed. A few years back when condo conversions were all the rage, an investor friend of mine invested in eight condos in one community. They had all been refurbished and were in an excellent area where he envisioned receiving substantial rents. The buying was made easy; he attended a "by invitation only" sales event where there were many other buyers and investors. He came prepared to purchase, and he was impressed with the properties

The problem was, he was a new investor who got caught up in the buying frenzy of the event. Although he had done comps in the area, and he believed the properties were priced reasonably, what he hadn't counted on was the 2008 catastrophic decline in the market. Suddenly he was stuck with eight properties that hadn't been over-priced until the market tanked. Now he didn't know how he was going to get rid of them.

Here's where his title officer came in to save the day. He insisted that all the agreements go through his title person, and since he was buying in volume, the sellers agreed. Because he wasn't a Realtor®, he didn't realize that there was an important piece of paperwork missing from the agreement. The sellers had not provided CC&Rs for him to review and authorize before signing the purchase agreement. And, the sellers, who builders, were also ignorant of the problem.

There were several Realtors® working the event, processing the agreements and giving the buyers their copies, and somehow nobody but the investor's title person noticed that there were no CC&Rs provided. Since this made the agreements voidable, the investor decided to take his option and void the contracts. Instead of getting stuck with the properties, the investor was released from all the contracts. Nobody wanted to have their licenses on the line for their failure to provide CC&Rs. All deposits were refunded, and the investor's title person was his new best friend. She saved him from losing a small fortune, and perhaps from having to fold operations altogether.

The reason I share this story is to illustrate how outstanding team members will end up saving you far more money than you'll spend. The partners you develop in your business have your back; they look out for you in their area of expertise. They will also let you know about any new ideas and innovative transactions that are being used by other Realtors® or investors.

• Property inspectors should also be a valuable member of the team. You need two inspectors—one who is willing to pick every little problem when it comes to purchasing a property, and the other who is more lenient when it comes to handling the selling end of the transaction. Both should provide accurate reports to deliver to the buyer; it just helps to have the two different styles of inspecting. The major repairs that need to be made will always need to be on an inspection report. It's just that some inspectors are easier going than others.

Of course, if you are dealing with a buyer's agent, the buyer will be the one to choose the inspector. One of the things many investors do is provide an inspection report with the property information. Many times, buyers are working on such a tight budget, they won't want to put out the extra $300 or $400 for an inspection. The inspection report is usually good for 30 days. Home inspectors who own their business are best. Again, you will always be talking to the decision maker.

- Decorators are crucial members of your team, and they should be contacted along with your contractor when you walk the property and decide what needs to be rehabbed. This is what will give your property that WOW factor we were talking about. You can find a good designer/decorator that can look at the property and see its potential. Their suggestions may cost you a little more short-term, but the long-term results will put money in your pocket.

Designers and decorators are often considered a luxury to have on a team, but that's because you aren't emotionally involved. When you need the buyers or renters to be emotionally involved, hire a designer or decorator up front. Some of the ideas they have offered have been incredible and attracted more people in the pool of buyers and tenants. Always ask what made the buyers or tenants choose your property, and you'll see that WOW factor created by designers and decorators will surface every time. Here are some of the things that have helped properties to sell without costing an arm and leg.

- o A dog run in the backyard

- o Changing a back patio into an atrium or closed in sunroom

- o Adding a closet to an office so it could qualify as an extra bedroom

- o Adding an outdoor kitchen and staging patio furniture for entertaining

- Closing in a courtyard, and adding a fireplace or water feature

- Making room in the kitchen for a double oven and some other gourmet touches

- Adding a gas line and including a gas stove and clothes dryer

- Covering up wall imperfections with a different paint color or some built-in shelving

- Adding blinds throughout the home

- Putting a spa in the backyard and surrounding it with a deck and plants

- Building a pergola and making the yard a small oasis with plants and a herb garden

- Stucco and paint ugly block fencing and adding a few planters filled with blooming plants

- Bumping a wall out and adding space to the master bath

- o Combining a formal living area and a family room to create one large living space

- o Putting shelving or storage bins in the garage

Staging the home is the last step in providing the WOW factor. A good stager will know exactly how to maximize space and draw attention to the details that will make your property memorable. Find one who has her own furniture and crew, so that you won't have to be bothered with the details.

When you show your properties to tenants or buyers, make it an event. Advertise it to the neighbors, to other Realtors®, and to some guests. Arrange a private showing before the big open house. Invite only the people who have worked with you and for you, and any buyers they have in mind. Everybody likes to have the advantage of being first to see a property.

Make sure your property appeals to all the senses. Remember, you're creating emotional appeal. It should look incredible, smell yummy, have textures and colors that make buyers and tenants want to sit for a while and enjoy the room. There should be soft music playing to relax your guests, and everybody should be treated like royalty, including Realtors® who are simply previewing the home.

If you are renting the property, you may want to stage it with your furniture and offer it as a furnished rental. This is especially useful if you are planning to use the home as an event location. Ah, and this brings up another idea for your investment portfolio. If you are investing in the major cities that cater to lots of entertaining or sporting events, find a property close to the event site and make it available for out-of-towners to rent the home instead of a hotel room. I've known investors to rent out an event home only two or three months of the year to event attendees, and make more than most landlords do over a 12 or 18-month period.

Then, they advertise it to other Realtors®, especially those selling new homes, for their buyers who need a three or four months furnished home. This can be quite attractive to buyers who don't want the bother of moving all their furniture and personal property two or three times. They can store it away and enjoy your beautiful property and all its amenities for a few short months while they are waiting for their homes to be built.

Of course, you're always going to need an excellent real estate attorney to call for advice and a real estate accountant as well. You don't need to keep them on your payroll, just know who to call when you need their help, or during tax time.

Lastly, if you are investing in over 20 properties a year, an excellent transaction coordinator is a must. You'll need him or her to be friendly, energetic and enthusiastic, attentive to details, and educated in investing and real estate. In some states, assistants don't have to be licensed real estate agents; they can provide information and use the MLS under the title of administrator. However, if they'll be showing property or writing agreements, they'll need to be licensed. An excellent transaction coordinator can be just the thing to make your property memorable when they know how to make your callers feel important and valued.

Some investors get around having their license because their transaction coordinators are licensed, and they use them to get access to Realtor® tools. Although it's one way to avoid getting licensed, it can be problematic, especially if things don't work out between the two of you. It's always a good idea to be able to work every aspect of your business if you had to, and then make it possible for you not to have to work it by yourself.

So, for the next properties, try to engage your emotions and look at things from a tenant's or buyer's perspective.

Chapter 4:
No Mercy Negotiations

Well, I suppose the title of this chapter got your attention, right? When you first started investing in real estate and negotiating transactions, you most likely wanted to build relationships and create a good rapport. So, you learned HOW to negotiate, and that's an excellent talent to have. Now that you know how to negotiate let's talk about knowing WHAT to negotiate. This is where the "no mercy" part comes into play.

Before you begin your belly-to-belly negotiations with the seller or buyer, you should have asked many questions. As you build that casual rapport, ask questions that seem innocent enough, but make them ones that will give you a lot of information when it comes to negotiating the agreement to your advantage. Here are some questions to ask, and the reasoning behind them.

Acting as the Seller of the Property

If you are selling the property, here are some of the questions you'll want to ask. Remember to appear casual, asking questions as if you were just making ordinary conversation instead of gathering information. Before you begin asking questions, be observant and give the buyers a chance to tell their story of why they are looking for a home. If they offer no conversation, then it's up to you to begin asking the questions that will give you the information you'll need when you get to the negotiations table.

- *So, why are you all looking for another house now?*

  If the weather is bad and the buyers are still out looking for a home, you can bet time is of the essence. After all, they have ventured out when other, less motivated buyers, would have put it off for another day or two. This sounds like a casual question that most buyers would have no problem answering, right? However, here is some information that a simple little question could provide you with information to be used in the negotiations.

  o My wife is pregnant—we need something bigger

  o I just got a raise—ready to step up

  o We don't like our neighborhood

o   I'm getting a divorce—need something more affordable

o   We want a pool, three-car garage, or any other amenity they desire—they want more upgrades or that WOW factor

How are you going to use this information in negotiating?   Easy, you're going to be the answer to their need or the solution to their problem. If there is a time constraint, such as the pregnancy, then when you are negotiating, remember that. Make it easy for them to close quickly. Instead of negotiating the price, negotiate the closing date, or you could let them move in before closing and do a lease back.

If they don't like the neighborhood they now live in, then talk to them about the HOA and how nicely it maintains the community. Negotiate the HOA fees, or offer to pay for or split the HOA transfer fees for the buyer. If you're going to do that, find out how much they are first. If they want a pool, you may want to offer in your negotiations free pool service for 60 days. Then send one of your vendors over to maintain the pool.

Anything you can negotiate besides the price of the home is good. Make up your mind far ahead of time that you will not reduce the price of the home, and then stick to it. Throw in a washer and dryer, or a refrigerator, pool service, storage in the garage, or your dog run in the backyard, which you had already created for a WOW, but don't cut your price. They don't have to know that the dog run was going to stay anyway. This is what is known as a "no mercy" negotiations—it's anything that's negotiable except the price.

The following are more questions you'll want to ask.

- When will you be looking to make a move?

- Will you be closer to your work from here?

- Oh, what is it that you do? (this will give you an idea of their financial status)

- Have you had a chance to look at the schools? Do they have kids? Will they be concerned about time in the negotiations—getting the home before school starts?

- Are you familiar with this area at all? Tout what your neighborhood has to offer. If they are not familiar with the area, they are probably not familiar with home values as well.

- Do you have friends that live out here?

- I noticed you're driving that big SUV, is your other vehicle that size too? (this would be a good one if you have an extended garage. You just want to remind them of the extras your home has when you negotiate. All those extras don't come cheap. Could they find a home for less? Probably! Would it have as many goodies? Probably not!)

No matter what questions you ask, make them count. Make your questions reveal information that can be used in negotiations.

If You Are Acting as the Buyer

The same holds true about the questions you ask as the purchaser. They should sound innocent and casual, but they should be the kind of questions that deliver a lot of negotiating information. Here are some to ask as the buyer.

- This is a lovely home; what did you like best about it when you bought it? (this builds rapport)

- So, do you have another place yet? This might mean they are more motivated to sell.

- I love your house—so, why are you all moving, anyway? This could indicate a financial issue, a divorce, an out-of-state move, or a change in family status. All those things will help you create urgency and perhaps a price reduction when it comes to the negotiations.

- Do you know if your loans are assumable by me if I decided to buy? (Make sure you say loans—as in plural—what you want to know is if they have a second mortgage on the home. When you say loans, you can even ask about their first and second loan, assuming they have two. They'll most likely say, "Oh, we only have one loan on the home, and I'm not sure if it can be assumed. I can find out for you if you like.") When you're looking for a home, it's always nice to find one where the seller has equity in case you want to try for a carryback. You should already know about the first loan, but there is no way of knowing whether they have taken out a second unless they volunteer the information. The records might show they have equity, but you won't know for sure unless you ask questions.

- If they have children's rooms that are crowded with toys, they might be looking for something bigger. That means, they may be willing to include some of the furnishings in the sale of the home if you are interested. They'll be wanting or needing bigger furniture for their new home. If they won't reduce the price of the home, then ask for the moon when it comes to furnishings.

Your primary goal as a buyer should be to get the sellers to reduce the home. This should be your "no mercy" point of the negotiations—a price reduction. Should you be a nice person in the process? Of course! Should you build rapport? Yes! People make more concessions for those they like, so like their home. Complement their taste in decorating, if you can be genuine. However, know the price you are willing to pay going into the negotiations, and DON"T BUDGE from that price. If the sellers are not willing to reduce the price, then be willing to walk.

One way to stick to your price is to choose a home that is above your price range so that your sellers will have to reduce the price or you won't be able to purchase the home. That is a "no mercy" negotiations.

Be an Active Listener

Listen to your opponent and continue the conversation by asking questions. Nod, agree and get them to agree. The more agreeable they are, the more likely they will be to agree with a price reduction. If they won't budge on price, then tempt them with a faster closing, or ask the sellers to pay for more items at closing. These are some of the things to ask for in place of a price reduction.

- $3,000 toward closing costs. It doesn't have to be $3,000; you name the price—it could be $5,000.

- The inspection costs. Offer to pay it up front, but be reimbursed at closing. You can do the same with the appraisal. That way it doesn't make them feel like they must take it out of their pocket. They just don't get as much at closing.

- Provide a two-year home warranty

- Leave the furnishings in the home that you desire

- Pay the HOA transfer fees, or HOA fees for six months

- Allow you to make renovations before closing and occupy the home without charging you a leaseback. This can be quite helpful if you are doing a flip.

Don't bully the sellers or buyers, but be firm about what you want. Find creative ways to negotiate. The "no mercy" way of negotiating means not giving yourself an out. Don't go back on what you previously agreed upon before entering the negotiations.

If you have left the table feeling like the negotiations was a piece of cake, then you didn't press hard enough. You should feel like you had to fight for what you want. If you didn't give it a good fight, then chances are you left some money or benefits on the table. Don't be afraid to press during the negotiations. You want to be considerate, but you're probably not going to become best friends. Your focus and concern should be on what you walk away with, not on making a new friend.

An investor I know says he always makes it a habit, when acting as the seller, to counter the first agreement with the same price. He just throws a little something in that he had planned to include anyway. Perfect "no mercy" negotiations.

At the end of the day, it's about the money, right? As much as you can, try to control every step of the transaction, especially the negotiations. Don't think negotiations begin at the end of the process; you are always negotiating with the seller or buyer to get them to agree with you. You're negotiating for the right to buy or sell the home, for the price, for what's included in that price, for how, when, and with whom it will be closed, for repairs, for closing costs, and for possession. As an investor, everything is negotiable.

Chapter 5:
Knowing When and How
to Say "NO"

Have you ever said "yes" to yourself and then regretted it the moment the word came out of your mouth? There is a time when all long-time investors learn the benefits of saying "no." Whether the "no" is to refuse the transaction altogether or to reject some condition of the sale. The difficult thing is to learn when and how to say "no," especially when you are negotiating an agreement.

If you know you must turn down an offer or try to make it sweeter, then always temper the "no" with a complement and an apology. For example; let's say you are the seller and the buyer is asking for everything including a heavy price reduction. You can say something like this: "You're quite the negotiator, aren't you? That would be a sweet deal if I could do it. I'm sorry, but we both know I have to say "no" to that. I'll tell you what, though, here's what I will do for you...." Now, you have tempered your refusal with a complement, an apology, and a token give. No hurt feelings; no sulky seller or buyer!

Here are some ways to recognize when you must say "no" to a transaction, even when you've let your emotions get in the way, and you want it badly.

Say "No" When Everything About the Transaction Has Been a Hassle

When everything goes south from the beginning, it typically doesn't get much better as time progresses. If you have a difficult buyer or seller, they tend to make the whole process more problems than it's worth. If the investment is this side of incredible, then it's worth a bit of worry, but just go into it knowing that it's going to be high maintenance.

When you move forward with a transaction that has been nothing but challenging from the get go, it's time to put your foot down and say no—and, NEXT. There are too many excellent investments around to put up with one that gives you heartburn. You'd be surprised; When you're ready to walk and show that you just don't care anymore, you can sometimes negotiate a smoking deal. It's okay to let the other person know you're fed up with the BS, and you're ready to walk. Then give a low-ball counter and tell them this is the end of it. Take it or leave it.

Say "No" When It's Outside Your Plan

You have a plan, and you've promised yourself you're going to stick with your plan. So, you must say "no" to anything that veers you from your goals. It could be an attractive investment, but it's outside your scope for now. Say "no!" Once you go down a rabbit hole in investing, there may be no getting back. The investment may go too deep and take up so much of your time that it diverts you from your success goals. Say "no!"

Say "No" When Your Inner Voice Tells You to Back Off

We've all ignored that inner voice in our head trying to direct us and give us advice. Most women have been taught to listen to their inner voice, but men brush it off and plow through most of the time. Stop, if only for a while, and give it a temporary "no" until you do what it takes to settle that voice of warning. That inner voice of warning was given to you for a reason; things usually turn out better when you're "all in."

Ask yourself why your self-talk is negative about this investment. Could it be your subconscious knows something you are refusing to see because your emotions are in the way? Perhaps the figures just don't add up, or you suspect the seller is not truthful. Whatever the cause, you must do what it takes to find out why your inner voice isn't on board with your decision.

Do what is needed to make that inner voice speak your concerns out loud. Talk things over with a fellow investor, or with your wife or your best friend. Once you hear yourself speak your fears or concerns out loud, you then begin to see if they have merit. It's good therapy to hear yourself work through an issue; you become your own counselor. If you've talked about it to your supporters and the concerns are still there, do yourself a favor and say "no."

Say "No" When You Can't Imagine Yourself Saying Yes

This might sound somewhat bizarre, but there have been times when people have said no because they just couldn't picture themselves being the owner of this property. It's important to envision your success as an investor, to imagine yourself owning this home or that building. If you can't see yourself as the owner, say "no."

I'm sure you've heard the stories of coaches who have challenged their teams into picturing themselves winning the game, or the season, and they've done it. Why? Because they could see themselves as winners. If you can't see yourself as a winner in the investment, don't play—say "no."

Say "No" When You're Counting on What Might Happen Instead of What Has Happened

Let the figures speak for themselves. If your due diligence tells you that this investment hasn't worked well for the last person, but you could do things much differently and have a huge turnaround, there's a good chance you should say "no." Not that you couldn't do a much better job of making the investment pay off, but if you're going to bet on future development or management, it better be reflected in an incredibly low price.

Say "No" If It Puts Other Properties in Jeopardy

If you must leverage everything to make this investment work, say "no." When you operate under such stress, it has an adverse effect on your health and your work. You are no longer able to negotiate to your advantage, because you're in a "need to" instead of "want to" position. If it creates a financial strain and causes you to be late on payments for other properties, then it hurts your relationship with your vendors. Suddenly, the trust it took so long to build is gone.

When your business is in jeopardy, your relationships will begin to sour, your confidence drops, your negotiations look desperate, and everything falls apart. For those of you who haven't been investing for long, you might be only one poor decision away from ruin. Investing is a crazy business, and not for the faint of heart, so say "no" to the deals that create undue stress that will make it difficult to conduct business as usual.

The great thing about saying "no," is the word after that will be "next." So, if this investment is too rich for your blood, or too heavy for you to carry for the time it requires, instead of just saying "no," say "next." There's always an investment right around the corner awaiting your expertise. Not every transaction is the right one. Even if it looks good on paper, and it promises to be profitable, it might not be the right one for you right now. There is value in knowing when to say "no" and to welcome the "next" opportunity.

Chapter 6:
When is the Best Time to Invest?

Investing in real estate is not like buying a car. It's commonly understood that the best time to purchase a new car from a dealership is at the end of the month when they are trying to fill their quotas. Car buyers also have learned to take advantage of end-of-the- year sales, when dealers want to move stock and prepare for new arrivals.

There is a time that is better than any other to invest in real estate as well. The best time is right now. You don't have to wait on the market because every market is a good one for real estate investors. If the market is right, properties are plenty, prices are reasonable, and qualifying for financing or raising private funding is possible. If the market is bad, prices are lower, interest rates are lower, and creative financing becomes the rage. The best time to invest isn't after you've read 100 books, talked to 20 other investors, asked 10 Realtors®, discussed it with all your friends, who understand little more about investing than you, or after you've saved thousands for a down payment.

Nope! All these obstacles you might be putting up are only excuses that can be easily overcome if the desire is there. For those of you who have been investing in one type of real estate for a long time and want to move into a different area—say from residential to commercial, the time to invest is now. You don't have to drop all your residential investments, just begin stepping into the commercial. Is there some preparation required? Yes! However, you've proven you can be a successful investor in one area of real estate, so practice the same steps as you enter another.

It's incredible how many people postpone greatness. They tell themselves when this or that happens, then I'll invest. For example; they say, "I'll invest when I get my real estate license." Or, "I'll move into commercial investments when I've built a portfolio of at least 10 successful residential investments." Or even, "I'll invest in commercial real estate when something comes along that I just can't refuse." Waiting for opportunity means just that—you're always waiting. Opportunity doesn't just happen, it is created. It is created by those who seek it, who find it and run with it. Great investors make great investments! Isn't it time you become one?

If you've been wanting to move from owning two investment properties to owning ten, you can do it. In fact, once you have a proven track record, you get properties at reduced prices, with less down, and at lower interest rates. Here's a little secret for you—increasing your investment activities by 100 percent doesn't mean doubling your efforts or money spent. The more you invest, the easier it becomes to create investment magic. Once you get a taste of success, you long for a repeat performance.

If your first investment was the pits, costing you a lot of money and heartburn, don't give up. You just haven't bridged the learning curve. Like any decision-making process, you'll get smarter and learn to make better deals in less time and with much less hassle. It's a numbers game. Many investors sell off their first few investments before they had intended because they recognize the possibilities to create better opportunities for their investment portfolios.

If you have stretched yourself to three investment properties, good for you. It's the stretching yourself that counts. Becoming a risk taker isn't the name of the game—it's becoming a CALCULATED risk taker that creates success. Don't jump in water that has an undercurrent and then hope you don't get buried by the pull lurking just below the surface. Expect and plan for what to do with what is going on beneath the surface of your next investment. Be prepared and ready. That's the best time to invest.

The best time to invest isn't when you inherit money; it's when you create a funding path. You may have to put a little more down and pay a little higher interest rate, but you've begun the process. Then, you can leverage the first investment to help you fund the second and third. Investing isn't just for retired people, or wealthy businessmen or women, it's for the ambitious 25-year-old who wants to make a name for him or herself in today's investment community. Investing in real estate is for the father to teach his son or daughter, helping them to be ready when they're old enough to sign an agreement legally. It starts that young.

In fact, investing in your future can begin as a youth, with parents teaching their children to set aside money from their weekly allowance. That's the problem with investing; kids have not been given the opportunity. Parents have failed to teach them as children how to become successful as adults. They may be risk takers by nature, but they don't know how to be CALCULATED risk takers. So, let's talk about that word "calculated."

Calculated Risk Takers Take It One Step at a Time

If you currently have three or four single-family rentals and are ready to take a calculated risk, you might decide to invest in a small multi-family dwelling. Perhaps a duplex or a four-plex would be a natural first step. If you have several single-family, and some multi-family units, you might want to take a calculated risk in a small retail strip center. The calculated risk takers don't make huge jumps, they test the waters and then do some wading first.

You may take a calculated risk and find that you don't want to take your business in that direction. So, you learned more about your long-term investment goals. That's a good thing. Or, you might enjoy the change and decide to swing your business in an entirely new direction. That's the beauty of being a real estate investor. It's up to you—it's your decision.

The thing with investing is that those who are willing to take risks must also calculate the possible loss and accept whatever consequences should come from their investment decisions. The raw facts about being willing to take the risk are that it's so much easier to say that when you've never experienced a dismal failure that can stop an eager investor in his or her tracks.

Every long-term real estate investor has made mistakes, and some that are so bad they make for entertaining party stories. You can count on the fact that you're no better than the best investors out there, and you're going to make your share of poor investments. It's how you weather the storm of that investment that will seal your fate as an investor. You know you must have an investment plan, but what about a plan that keeps you afloat should an investment fail?

Weathering a Failed Investment

When making it through a poor investment decision, or an unexpected turn for the worse, practice the three Rs.

Refocus

Take another look at the initial plan for the investment. Perhaps there's still a chance to salvage your money if you refocus your efforts. It may not be a short-term investment as first expected, but require a longer ride to give you a better return on your investment. Look at what else you can do to recoup your money. Get creative; think of innovative ideas that might change the outcome of this investment. It may mean a different exit strategy. Instead of renting the property for a year, try short-term rentals and market it to companies who might use your property.

Restructure

If it's a commercial property, perhaps you think of some creative way to attract more tenants. Turn them into month-by-month leases with higher rents. Offer long-term tenants a lease with no security deposit and agree to do their buildouts. Just restructure the terms that were in your initial plan. Again, get creative.

Recommit

It is so tempting to dump a failed investment and take a loss just to rid yourself of the headache. However, you might be missing a tremendous opportunity. At this point, you've probably got more to lose by dumping the property than you do by recommitting yourself to making a go of it. Set a time limit for success, and throw yourself into making a success of it. Recommit yourself to finding a way to make it work. If at the end of your deadline, the property is still a failure, then it's time to say "NEXT."

What are you waiting for—get out there and invest! There's no time better than the present.

Conclusion

Thank you for making it through to the end of *Rental Property Millionaire: The Ultimate Crash Course on Rental Property Investing.* Let's hope it was informative and able to provide you with all of the tools you need to achieve your real estate investment goals.

The next step is to take your investing endeavors to the next level. You have skillfully managed a few investments, so it's time to step up to greater heights of success. If you want to continue to stretch yourself, to learn new investment strategies that help your business to grow, then you can't let a few setbacks sidetrack you from your initial goals.

You may have done a great job persuading others to trust you, but now it's time to trust yourself. Make that next investment decision with confidence. If you've learned new things to do before investing this time, try them. Develop an investment plan and then write down your goals and some step-by-step processes to achieve those goals. Decide on an exit strategy before you even shop for the property; that will help you determine what property will be perfect for this investment opportunity.

Also, try to look at what you're purchasing from a buyer's or renter's perspective, and invest in a property that has the potential for creating the WOW. Engage your buyer's eye when you purchase your next investment. Look back over some of the questions we discussed, and don't be shy about making conversation with the sellers and the Realtors®. You'll be surprised at all the information you get when you chat them up.

Investing is an exciting adventure, so if you've lost your initial enthusiasm, try another type of investing. Take your business to the next level. Try more upper-end properties or multi-family dwellings. Or, take a chance on learning about commercial investing. Find a mentor who will teach you and, in return, partner with them in a commercial investment opportunity to walk you through the process.

If your business has grown stale, it's most likely your interest has waned, so engage—go "all in" on something that intrigues and challenges you. What separates real estate investment from other passive income is that, first of all, it isn't passive. The people you meet and the things you do each day should be creative and push you to learn and excel in different skills and strategies. So, welcome the challenges and look at them as opportunities to learn and grow.

Thank you again for reading *Rental Property Millionaire: The Ultimate Crash Course on Rental Property Investing.* Let me know how it helped you become a better real estate investor by posting a review on Amazon and good luck with all your future investments.

Finally, for additional resources on making money in Real Estate, please remember to check out the following books on our Amazon Author page:

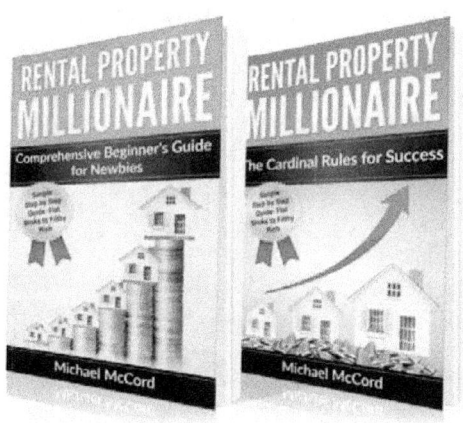

https://www.amazon.com/ Michael-McCord/e/B01LYIFPLO/ ref=dp_byline_cont_ebooks_1

https://www.amazon.com/
Michael-McCord/e/B01LYIFPLO/
ref=dp_byline_cont_ebooks_1

https://www.amazon.com/
Michael-McCord/e/B01LYIFPLO/
ref=dp_byline_cont_ebooks_1

https://www.amazon.com/
Michael-McCord/e/B01LYIFPLO/
ref=dp_byline_cont_ebooks_1

https://www.amazon.com/
Michael-McCord/e/B01LYIFPLO/
ref=dp_byline_cont_ebooks_1

THANK YOU AGAIN AND BEST OF LUCK!!